D1365966

The Cold War in the Middle East 1950–1991

The Cold War in the Middle East 1950–1991

Brent E. Sasley

Mason Crest Publishers
Philadelphia

Frontispiece: Afghan resistance fighters holding U.S.-supplied weapons, circa 1988.

Produced by OTTN Publishing, Stockton, N.J.

Mason Crest Publishers
370 Reed Road
Broomall, PA 19008
www.masoncrest.com

Printed and bound in Malaysia.

First printing

1 3 5 7 9 8 6 4 2

Library of Congress Cataloging-in-Publication Data

Sasley, Brent E.
The cold war in the Middle East, 1950–1991 / Brent E. Sasley.
p. cm. — (The making of the Middle East)
Includes bibliographical references and index.
ISBN-13: 978-1-4222-0173-2
ISBN-10: 1-4222-0173-2
1. Middle East—Foreign relations—Soviet Union—Juvenile literature. 2. Soviet Union—Foreign relations—Middle East—Juvenile literature. 3. Cold War—Juvenile literature. I. Title.

DS63.2.S65S27 2007
956.04—dc22

2007028959

Arab-Israeli Relations, 1950–1979

The Arabian Peninsula in the Age of Oil

The Cold War in the Middle East, 1950–1991

The Iranian Revolution and the Resurgence of Islam

The Middle East in the Age of Uncertainty, 1991–Present

The Ottoman and Qajar Empires in the Age of Reform

The Palestine Mandate and the Creation of Israel, 1920–1949

The Rise of Nationalism: The Arab World, Turkey, and Iran

Tensions in the Gulf, 1978–1991

Table of Contents

(Opposite) An oil tanker plies the waters of the Persian Gulf. (Right) President Franklin D. Roosevelt talks with Abd al-Aziz ibn Saud, king of Saudi Arabia, 1945. Roosevelt promised the king military assistance in return for secure access to Saudi oil. The Middle East's vast reserves of petroleum—the lifeblood of industrial economies—made it a region of enormous strategic importance.

1 Introduction: Roots of the Struggle

By the conclusion of World War II (1939–1945), two countries had emerged as the globe's preeminent powers: the United States and the Union of Soviet Socialist Republics, or Soviet Union. The two superpowers had been wartime allies, but after the defeat of Nazi Germany and Imperial Japan, their relationship quickly degenerated into one of mutual suspicion, competition, and confrontation. For more than four decades, the United States and the Soviet Union would be locked in an ideological struggle that came to be called the Cold War. This struggle reached into all regions of the globe, as each superpower attempted to enlist allies to its side and to undermine its adversary. Underpinning the Cold War were incompatible political and economic systems: liberal democracy and free-market capitalism in the U.S.-led West versus authoritarian rule and state-controlled economies in the Soviet-controlled Communist bloc. While the United States and the Soviet Union never went to war against each other directly, they supported opposing sides in various regional conflicts.

The Cold War didn't begin in the Middle East, but the region became a key battleground in the superpowers' struggle for global supremacy. In fact, events in the Middle East would bring the United States and the Soviet Union to the brink of nuclear confrontation in 1973.

Quest for Oil

Although the Cold War drew the superpowers into increased involvement in the Middle East, the United States and the Soviet Union both had strategic and economic interests in the region that predated their rivalry. The primary American concern, before the Cold War, was oil.

By 1917 the United States produced two-thirds of the world's total oil output. Nevertheless, during the 1920s American policymakers began to worry that domestic production of this increasingly vital resource would dry up. The solution, they concluded, was to find foreign sources. The United States thus joined in the search for Middle Eastern oil, which until then had been dominated by the British. Britain had been the primary beneficiary of large oil fields discovered in Persia (present-day Iran) in 1908. After petroleum was discovered in Saudi Arabia 30 years later, American companies assumed a central role in developing Saudi oil fields.

Fears that the United States would run out of oil resurfaced during World War II. Again American policymakers concluded that the protection of foreign sources was critical. At this point, however, American policy on obtaining oil in the Middle East brought the United States into economic competition with Britain, a staunch political ally. The United States favored an "open door" policy in the region, which meant that no country would have special privileges when it came to investing in regional economic activity. Such a policy seemed fair, but it proved most favorable to the United States, which was in the strongest position after the war to invest in developing the region's resources.

Securing an Empire

In contrast to the United States, whose pre–Cold War involvement in the Middle East was motivated overwhelmingly by the acquisition of oil, the Soviet Union had varied strategic interests in the region. In fact, the Middle East was a focus of Russian foreign policy long before the 1922 establishment of the Union of Soviet Socialist Republics. The czars—who had ruled Russia for three centuries before the Russian Revolution of 1917 ended their reign—had always believed in the military necessity and destiny of Russia to expand its empire through Central Asia and into the Middle East, particularly into Iran. The Communists of the Soviet era shared this belief.

However, the incorporation into the Russian Empire of the Islamic kingdoms of Central Asia presented problems for the czars, as well as for their

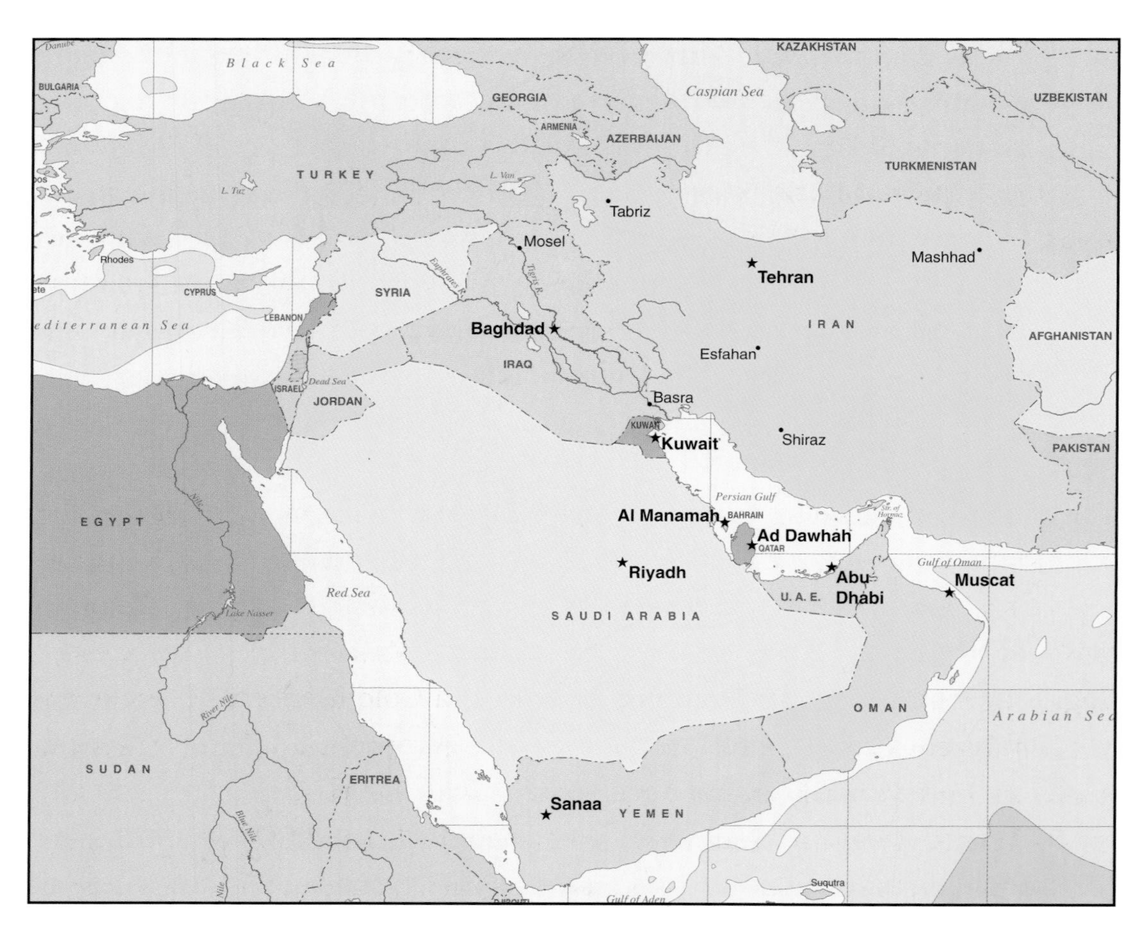

The heart of the Middle East.

Communist successors. The primary concern was that Central Asian Muslims, responding to appeals from their co-religionists in the Middle East, might rebel against Russian (or Soviet) authority. Gaining influence in Turkey, Iran, and Afghanistan would help protect against this possibility. It would also help prevent other powers (primarily the British) from using these countries as springboards into Central Asia.

Another main objective of Russian foreign policy, since the 17th century, was the acquisition of a warm-water port that would remain unfrozen and open for the entire year. This would allow Russian commercial and military vessels to move more easily around the world. The most viable location was at the Turkish Straits, the twisting waterway that cuts through Turkey and connects the Black Sea to the Mediterranean Sea.

Shifting Priorities

The coming of the Cold War caused the superpowers to modify their strategic thinking vis-à-vis the Middle East. For the United States, the major priority was to prevent any expansion of Soviet influence in the region; all other goals were subordinated to this one. In fact, Washington rarely viewed regional politics through anything other than a Cold War lens. Every event was analyzed in terms of how it undermined or contributed to the American position, and virtually every development that undermined the American position was viewed as resulting from Communist manipulation. Secondary U.S. goals in the Middle East included ensuring a stable supply of oil from the Persian Gulf, maintaining lines of communication, and protecting Israel and the pro-Western Arab states.

For its part, the Soviet Union sought to undercut the United States and extend its own influence in the Middle East. But, as Soviet policymakers fully recognized, the United States enjoyed distinct advantages, including strong relationships with key states (such as Saudi Arabia and Israel) and military bases in the Persian Gulf. In addition to protecting its "soft underbelly" in Central Asia, the Soviets desired to outflank the West, which had direct access—via Turkey—to Soviet borders in the Caucasus region.

It is important to note that, despite the significant impact of the Cold War on Middle Eastern politics, developments in the Middle East were not dictated by the superpower competition only. In fact, local leaders proved quite adept at using the superpowers' rivalry to their own advantage. Many Middle Eastern states obtained considerable amounts of aid from the United States or the Soviet Union—in some cases even shifting their loyalties according to their specific needs at the time.

Crises in Iran and Turkey

Superpower competition in the Middle East began in the area called the northern tier—the countries that comprise the northern boundaries of the region: Iran and Turkey.

The Soviet Union had established a presence in Iran during World War II. In August 1941, fearing the pro-Nazi leanings of Iran's shah, or king, Soviet and British troops invaded and occupied the country. By the terms of a treaty signed in 1942, however, Britain and the Soviet Union agreed to withdraw all troops from Iranian territory within six months of the war's end. The British lived up to their obligations, but the Soviet Union balked.

Instead of leaving Iranian Azerbaijan, in the north of the country, Soviet forces—in collusion with the local Marxist party (the Tudeh)—began agitating for autonomy for the area. In November 1945 a Tudeh-linked group announced the establishment of an independent government in Iranian

Azerbaijan. An autonomous Kurdish republic was proclaimed a month later in northwestern Iran. Both were Soviet puppet regimes. The Soviet Red Army prevented Iranian troops from entering these areas and reasserting the central government's authority there.

These actions increased American suspicions of the Soviet Union. The United States, along with Great Britain, kept up steady pressure on the Soviet leadership to honor the commitments it had made in 1942. That pressure—in combination with Iranian promises to consider Soviet requests for access to Iran's oil—finally led to the pullout of Soviet forces in May 1946. By the end of the year the central government in Tehran had succeeded in reestablishing its control over the north, and few traces of Soviet influence in the country remained.

Soviet leader Joseph Stalin, photographed around 1942. Stalin's post–World War II territorial demands on Turkey alarmed U.S. policymakers and helped spawn the Cold War.

Meanwhile, the Soviet Union seemed to be adopting an aggressive posture toward Turkey. In 1945 Soviet leader Joseph Stalin demanded the return of Kars and Ardahan, two regions that had been ceded to Turkey in a 1921 treaty. Stalin later demanded that Turkey permit the construction of Soviet military bases at the Turkish Straits, and that the Soviet Union be granted joint control of the strategic waterway.

The U.S. president, Harry S Truman, opposed these demands. In a blunt message to his Soviet counterpart, Truman dispatched the most powerful battleship in the U.S. Navy, the *Missouri,* to the Turkish Straits in 1946.

Stalin eventually withdrew his demands. But American policymakers remained deeply concerned about what they saw as the Soviet Union's continuing efforts to subvert the independence of Turkey. Nor was it clear that Moscow's designs on Iran had been definitively thwarted. If the Soviet Union succeeded in gaining a foothold in the northern tier, American oil interests in Saudi Arabia might be threatened.

Before World War II, Great Britain had sought to protect large parts of the eastern Mediterranean and Middle East regions—including Greece, Turkey, Iran, and the Persian Gulf states—from external encroachment. Some of this grew out of the "Great Game"—the struggle for influence in Central Asia between the British and Russian empires. Britain wanted to keep open the land and sea routes to its most important colony, India. Later, protecting its access to Middle East oil became a high priority.

Many U.S. policymakers would have been content to see Britain continue its role in guaranteeing security in the eastern Mediterranean and Middle East. However, after World War II, Britain was exhausted and devastated. By early 1947, in the midst of an extremely harsh winter, the country faced economic collapse. Militarily and financially, Britain could no longer sustain all its far-reaching commitments.

On February 21, 1947, the British ambassador in Washington delivered a message informing American officials of his country's intention to end its commitments in the eastern Mediterranean. This, U.S. policymakers understood, would place two countries in imminent jeopardy of Communist subversion: Turkey and Greece, which was then in the midst of a civil war. And, American officials reasoned, Communist successes in Turkey and Greece might open up the Middle East—as well as Western Europe and North Africa—to Soviet expansion. The United States would have to take decisive action to contain the Soviet threat.

The Truman Doctrine

On March 12, 1947, President Truman delivered a speech before the U.S. Congress, outlining what came to be known as the Truman Doctrine. "At the present moment in world history nearly every nation must choose between alternative ways of life," Truman declared.

> One way of life is based upon the will of the majority, and is distinguished by free institutions, representative government, free elections, guarantees of individual liberty, freedom of speech and religion, and freedom from political oppression.
>
> The second way of life is based upon the will of a minority forcibly imposed upon the majority. It relies upon terror and oppression, a controlled press and radio; fixed elections, and the suppression of personal freedoms.

Under the administration of President Harry Truman, containment of Communist expansion became the central goal of U.S. foreign policy.

The Middle East Divided

It is not completely accurate to say that every country in the Middle East aligned itself with either the pro-American or pro-Soviet bloc during the Cold War. After 1979 Iran, for example, was openly hostile toward both superpowers. Other countries—most prominently Egypt until the mid-1970s—shifted allegiances between the two blocs in order to maximize the support received. But aside from these few exceptions, most countries in the region did identify consistently with one camp over the other.

States that openly sided with the United States included Saudi Arabia, Iran before 1979, Jordan, Turkey, Israel, and Egypt after 1974. In addition, the smaller Persian Gulf monarchies (Kuwait, Bahrain, Qatar, the United Arab Emirates, and Oman) and Morocco were pro-American but without the overt affiliation exemplified by Saudi Arabia.

The countries that joined the Soviet camp—often referred to as the revolutionary or radical states—were Syria, Egypt between 1955 and 1973, Libya, Algeria, Yemen, and Iraq (though it also tried to obtain American support, particularly military aid). The Palestine Liberation Organization (a militant-terrorist group committed to destroying Israel and replacing it with a Palestinian state) was also in the Soviet camp.

Both superpowers, however, often had trouble controlling or directing their allies. On many occasions the Middle Eastern states went against their patrons' wishes or even engaged in policies that harmed them. Saudi Arabia, for example, joined a 1973–1974 oil embargo against the United States, to protest American support of Israel. The embargo caused oil and gasoline prices to jump, producing a major shock to the American economy.

The "second way of life" was a clear reference to Soviet-style communism, and Truman declared that the United States would actively oppose its spread. "I believe that it must be the policy of the United States," he declared, "to support free peoples who are resisting attempted subjugation by armed minorities or by outside pressures."

The president asked Congress for $400 million to help Greece and Turkey fend off Communist subversion. If these countries fell, he said, "confusion and disorder might well spread throughout the entire Middle East."

The lines had been drawn. The United States would resist Soviet efforts to expand Communist influence. There could be no compromise in this kind of struggle.

By the end of the 1940s, U.S. aid had helped stabilize Greece and Turkey. Iran, too, appeared to be firmly in the Western camp.

The Establishment of Israel

Thwarted in the northern tier, Soviet leaders looked for other opportunities to expand their country's influence in the Middle East. The establishment of Israel, on May 14, 1948, seemed to provide an opening. Soviet leaders believed they had a natural ideological ally, as many of Israel's founders were staunch socialists. But support for Israel had more to do with weakening British and American influence in the region. The Soviets provided weapons to help Israel in its 1947–1949 war against the Arabs. Relations would sour in 1950, however, when Israel supported the American action in the Korean War.

As the 1950s progressed, the superpowers' struggle for influence in the Middle East would intensify. The Cold War in the region was heating up.

(Opposite) Soviet premier Nikita Khrushchev (at left) shakes hands with Gamal Abdel Nasser, president of Egypt. In the mid-1950s Nasser turned to the Communist bloc to obtain weapons, alienating the United States. (Right) Iranian soldiers and tanks in the streets of Tehran following the August 19, 1953, coup that ousted Mohammad Mossadeq, Iran's prime minister.

2 The 1950s: The Cold War Heats Up

Although both the United States and the Soviet Union became more involved in the Middle East during the late 1940s, Great Britain and France retained significant influence in the region. Indeed, these two countries, each of which had a historic role as colonizers in the Middle East, remained the region's dominant external powers. That would not be the case by the end of the 1950s. In its effort to stop Soviet infiltration in the Middle East, the United States began to assume a more direct role in shaping events there. For its part, the Soviet Union would capitalize on a major opportunity during the 1950s to make inroads in the Arab world's most important state.

The Nationalization of Iran's Oil Industry

The importance of Iran, in the context of the Cold War, had first been recognized by American policymakers in 1946, after Soviet efforts to create puppet regimes in the north. But a political crisis in Iran from 1950 to 1953 drew the United States even deeper into Iranian affairs, and marked the beginning of a U.S.-Iranian alliance that would last a quarter century.

Mohammad Mossadeq championed the nationalization of Iranian oil assets. He also sought support from a Marxist party, the Tudeh. Both actions marked him for removal by the Eisenhower administration.

In 1941, after the Soviets and British had forced the shah from power to forestall an Iranian alliance with Nazi Germany, they placed his 21-year-old son, Mohammed Reza Pahlavi, on the throne. The new shah oppressed critics of his reign and sought to keep the old elites in power. His actions generated intense opposition from much of Iranian society. By the late 1940s this opposition coalesced into the National Front political party, led by Mohammad Mossadeq. A popular politician, Mossadeq championed an objective shared by most Iranians—an end to foreign interference in Iranian politics and foreign domination of Iran's economy, particularly the oil industry. This inevitably meant opposition to the shah, who was seen as having facilitated and maintained foreign domination.

In 1950 the Iranian government negotiated a new agreement with the Anglo-Iranian Oil Company (AIOC), the British-controlled company that dominated Iranian oil exploitation. The agreement was submitted to the Majlis, Iran's parliament, for approval. Mossadeq rallied opposition to the agreement because the pact would still leave control of oil exploitation in foreign hands. In March 1951, after negotiations to create an acceptable arrangement had failed, the Majlis voted to nationalize the AIOC. The following month, with overwhelming support in the Majlis and among the Iranian people, Mossadeq was appointed prime minister.

Britain responded by imposing economic sanctions on Iran, including an embargo that prevented the country from exporting its oil. Behind the scenes, the British intelligence service also began planning a coup to oust Mossadeq.

The British embargo took a severe toll on the Iranian economy, which in turn created widespread unrest. The once-popular National Front began to lose its appeal. Mossadeq turned to the Iranian Marxist party, the Tudeh, to bolster his nationalist movement. Many Iranians started to see the Tudeh as the best choice for stabilizing the country.

These developments alarmed American officials, who believed the Soviet Union would gain great influence in Iran if the Tudeh came to power. The U.S. Central Intelligence Agency (CIA), with aid from British intelligence, plotted a coup.

Matters came to a head in August 1953. In keeping with the CIA plan, the shah attempted to replace Mossadeq, but the prime minister refused to step down. Large crowds of Mossadeq supporters took to the streets of Tehran, and pro-shah military and security officers—whom the CIA had been counting on to support the coup—failed to turn out. The shah hastily fled the country. It appeared that Mossadeq had triumphed.

On August 19, however, Iranians working for the CIA succeeded in mustering pro-shah mobs. These mobs marched on the parliament building and attacked the offices of several pro-Mossadeq newspapers. Soon pro-shah army units and security forces had deployed throughout Tehran. Mossadeq was arrested (he was later convicted of treason), and on August 22 the shah returned to Iran.

The successful coup represented the first direct involvement of the United States in the Middle East. Previous American involvement had been based only on public warnings and the provision of aid.

In the wake of his close brush with being overthrown, the shah repressed his domestic critics even more harshly. He also became one of the staunchest supporters of U.S. interests in the region. Over the years he spent billions of dollars on advanced American weapons systems. U.S. policymakers would rely on his regime to be a bulwark against Soviet infiltration in the region—and he relished that role.

The Czech-Egyptian Arms Deal

In 1952 a group of army officers led by Gamal Abdel Nasser overthrew the Egyptian monarchy. The Free Officers, as they called themselves, made clear that they preferred American support over Soviet aid. Nasser (who became Egypt's president in 1954) and his colleagues believed that only the United States could provide their country the economic aid it needed. They further believed that the United States could pressure its close ally Britain into leaving the region. The Free Officers also regarded communism with considerable suspicion.

But Egypt needed something that the United States wasn't willing to provide: arms. As part of the Tripartite Declaration of May 25, 1950, the United States—along with France and Britain—had agreed not to sell any weapons that could be used offensively to Israel or any Arab country. The goal had been to dampen the Arab-Israeli conflict.

In February 1955 Britain signed a military agreement, the Baghdad Pact, with Turkey, Iraq, Iran, and Pakistan. President Nasser and other Egyptian leaders perceived this as a Western effort to control the region's security—and they believed it had American support. Resentment over the issue helped push Egyptian leaders to

Gamal Abdel Nasser, who rose to power after the 1952 Free Officers' coup overthrew Egypt's monarchy, tried to steer clear of committing to either the Soviet or the American side. Instead he attempted to play the Cold War adversaries against each other and obtain benefits from both.

seek another source for the weapons the Western powers had been unwilling to supply. The final straw was the Americans' hesitation in providing financial backing for the Aswan High Dam, a major development project championed by Nasser. The Soviet Union sensed an opportunity.

In September 1955 Czechoslovakia, under Moscow's orders, sold $200 million worth of advanced weaponry to Egypt in exchange for cotton. As a result of the Czech-Egyptian arms deal, the Soviet Union had gotten a foothold in Middle Eastern politics—to the detriment of the United States. By 1956 the Soviets had further capitalized on this opening and become the primary supplier of weapons to Syria as well.

American officials weren't pleased with Nasser's arms purchases. They were further angered when Egypt extended official diplomatic recognition to Communist China. On July 19, 1956, the United States withdrew funding for the Aswan High Dam. A week later, Nasser announced the nationalization of the Suez Canal, which had been run by a Paris-based company with British and French shareholders.

The Suez Crisis Sparks War

The Suez Canal, which had effectively been under British control since 1882, generated significant revenue for the British government. It was also of great strategic importance. Its loss constituted a severe blow to British finances, prestige, and influence. Officials in the British government began making plans to undermine Nasser and regain control of the Suez Canal.

But the British government wasn't alone in wanting to take action against Nasser's Egypt. Israeli officials worried about the military buildup

Egypt had begun with the Czech-Egyptian arms deal. Believing that the balance of power in the region was tipping dangerously against their country, they sought a way to weaken Nasser's armed forces before Egypt had the upper hand. For their part, French officials considered an Egyptian-controlled Suez Canal a serious setback to their national interests. They were also angry over what they believed to be Nasser's support for rebels fighting to end French colonial rule in Algeria.

By October 1956 the British, French, and Israeli governments had agreed on a secret plan to deal with Egypt. On October 29 the Israeli army invaded the Sinai Peninsula and drove rapidly toward the Suez Canal. Invoking a 1954 Anglo-Egyptian treaty that gave Britain the right to intervene militarily in the Suez Canal Zone in the event of a war, the British and French demanded that Israeli and Egyptian forces pull back 10 miles (16 kilometers) from the Canal. Nasser refused. British and French warplanes pounded Egyptian targets, while an Anglo-French force landed in Egypt on November 5. The Egyptian military was quickly routed, and by November 6 the Suez was under the control of the Anglo-French force. The Suez Campaign of the British, French, and Israelis had apparently been an unqualified success.

Headlines from various British newspapers for October 31, 1956, announce the Anglo-French military operation to secure the Suez Canal.

President Dwight D. Eisenhower was furious at the British, French, and Israelis for their collusion in precipitating the Suez Crisis. Facing Soviet threats of a military response, and worried about perceptions of the United States in the Third World, Eisenhower pressured the British and French to withdraw from the Suez Canal Zone by the end of 1956. The Israelis withdrew from Sinai the following March.

However, far from being politically weakened or removed from power, as the British and French had hoped, Nasser emerged from the Suez war as a hero among Arabs and among people in the Third World generally. He had stood up to the Western powers and refused to give in to their demands.

More important, the superpowers became involved in the Suez Crisis. The Soviet Union threatened to send troops into the Suez Canal Zone, or even to attack France and England directly. In Washington, President Dwight D. Eisenhower moved to avert a showdown with the Soviet Union. Eisenhower had been surprised and outraged by the Suez invasion; the British and French, allies of the United States, had not informed Washington of their plans. Eisenhower placed sanctions on Britain, France, and Israel, and he pushed for the deployment of a United Nations force to separate the opposing armies.

Eisenhower recognized that the invasion had put the United States in an extremely difficult position, and not simply because of the risk of a direct military confrontation with the Soviet Union. A day before British and French troops landed in Egypt, Soviet troops had invaded Hungary. The United States had strongly condemned that aggression; it could hardly condone a similar action by its allies. Moreover, officials in the Eisenhower administration feared that the United States would be identified with the Europeans since they were allies. This would undermine the U.S. position in the Middle East—and the Third World more broadly—and it might pave the way for the Soviets to claim the right of intervention as well.

Under intense American pressure, the British and French withdrew from the Suez Canal Zone by the end of 1956. Israel pulled its soldiers from the Sinai Peninsula the following March. The resolution of the Suez Crisis signaled the further decline of British and French influence in the Middle East. The United States was clearly the dominant Western power in the region, and it would bear full responsibility for fending off Soviet advances.

The Eisenhower Doctrine

That responsibility was formally acknowledged in a speech to Congress President Eisenhower delivered on January 5, 1957. The speech contained what became known as the Eisenhower Doctrine. If the Truman Doctrine was meant to apply American aid to the eastern Mediterranean area, the Eisenhower Doctrine was intended to encompass the entire Middle East.

Eisenhower warned that "International Communism" was trying to take advantage of recent instabilities in the Middle East and that Congress should "authorize such assistance and cooperation to include the employment of the armed forces of the United States to secure and protect the territorial integrity and political independence of such nations, requesting such aid, against overt armed aggression from any nation controlled by International Communism." The United States would, in other words, give outright military support to any country threatened by Soviet advances. This was the clearest statement yet that the United States was absolutely committed to keeping the Soviet Union out of the region.

U.S. policymakers hoped that, by strengthening friendly Arab regimes, the Eisenhower Doctrine would limit the pan-Arab appeal of Gamal Abdel Nasser—and perhaps even weaken the Egyptian president domestically. However, the doctrine never won widespread support among regional states. Its military provisions were applied only once, in Lebanon. A political crisis there and a revolution in Iraq, which overthrew the pro-Western monarchy, stoked American fears of a general disruption of American interests and of a region-wide Communist takeover. The Lebanese president, Camille Chamoun, played upon these American fears to drag the United States into the country to support his bid for reelection. He argued that Egypt, under Soviet manipulation, was trying to undermine the pro-Western orientation of Lebanon. Anxious to remind the Soviets of American commitments to defend the region from communism, President Eisenhower dispatched a contingent of Marines to Lebanon on July 15, 1958. The Lebanese situation stabilized, though only partly due to the American presence, and the Marines withdrew by October.

Conclusion

If the end of the 1940s saw the introduction of Cold War politics into the Middle East, the 1950s witnessed deepening superpower involvement in the region, including direct intervention. The 1950s also saw the beginning of the U.S.-Soviet competition over Egypt, which would continue into the mid-1970s.

(Opposite) At a military parade in Cairo, Egyptian servicemen stand at attention as Soviet-made antitank guns pass by. The 1960s witnessed a major arms race in the Middle East, with the Soviet Union and the United States providing advanced weapons to their regional allies. (Right) Dead Egyptian soldiers in the Sinai Peninsula during the Six-Day War, June 1967.

3 The 1960s: The Arab-Israeli Conflict Intensifies

As the 1950s ended, the Soviet Union had achieved a presence in the Middle East through its arms sales to Egypt and Syria, and the United States had become more deeply involved through its commitment to defend the region from Soviet advances. In the 1960s the superpowers competed for the loyalty of Egypt, which both regarded as the key player in the Middle East. This enabled Egyptian policymakers to play the superpowers off against each other.

During the 1960s the U.S. relationship with Israel also became closer, which drew the United States deeper into the Arab-Israeli conflict. That conflict assumed greater importance, for both regional and Cold War politics.

The Struggle for Egypt

During the 1950s and 1960s, Egypt was the most important country in the Middle East. The most populous Arab country, it also had one of the Arab world's strongest militaries, making it a key state in the confrontation with Israel. Moreover, the charismatic Gamal Abdel Nasser enjoyed great popularity across the Arab world because of his fiery rhetoric and refusal to submit to the demands of either superpower. In fact, in many Arab countries Nasser was more popular among ordinary people than were the actual leaders of those countries. All of this made Egypt crucial to the superpowers' struggle for regional influence.

After the Free Officers' coup in 1952, Egypt's new leaders had been quite clear about their preference for American aid. But Nasser was also determined to avoid dependence on either of the superpowers. Strongly opposed to any hint of colonialism, he wanted Egypt's foreign policy to be completely independent. Although he recognized that in the context of the Cold War he would be pressured to publicly ally himself with one side or the other, Nasser was convinced that he could successfully navigate between the two superpowers without committing himself to either. Moreover, he personally aspired to regional leadership, and in that quest there could be no place for knuckling under to superpower demands.

The United States was perceived to be the least imperialist of the Western powers. Unlike Britain and France, it did not have an extensive history of colonialism, and furthermore it could provide the kind of financial and economic aid that Egypt needed. However, because the United States subordinated all of its Middle Eastern policies to its overall Cold War agenda, it was unwilling to provide aid unless Nasser explicitly agreed to help enhance the American position in the region while keeping the Soviets out. Nasser's nonalignment was not good enough—Egypt had to be firmly in the Western camp if it was to receive U.S. aid.

Nasser would not to agree to this. In addition, tensions erupted between Egypt and the United States—particularly under the administration of President Lyndon Johnson (1963–1969)—as a result of several developments in the early and mid-1960s. These developments included Egyptian support for the republicans against the Saudi-supported royalists in the Yemeni civil war; public Egyptian harangues against American support for Jordan, Saudi Arabia, and Israel; and personal animosity between Nasser and Johnson. The United States slowly reduced its aid commitments to Egypt; by 1965 it had discontinued all aid.

Nasser was left with little choice but to turn to the Soviet Union. Moscow was only too eager to supply military and economic aid to Egypt. After the failure to achieve its goals in Turkey and Iran in 1946, bringing Egypt to its side would mean a successful leap over the northern tier directly into the heart of the Middle East. Moreover, although the Soviets considered the Czech-Egyptian arms deal of 1955 a stepping-stone into the region, they were disappointed that Nasser still preferred American aid and only took Soviet support because he could not get it elsewhere. Now it appeared that the Egyptian-American break was complete, and that the Soviet Union had Egypt all to itself. For Moscow, good relations with Egypt were the key to undermining the U.S. position in the region and expanding the Soviet Union's influence in the Third World—which was seen as necessary in the overall Cold War competition.

The Middle Eastern Arms Race

The 1960s also witnessed an intensifying arms race between Israel and the Arab states, and between Egypt and Syria, on the one hand, and Saudi Arabia on the other. The 1950 Tripartite Declaration had committed the United States (and Britain and France) to providing only arms that were necessary for internal security and self-defense. The United States therefore refused, for much of the 1950s, to sell offensive weapons to either Israel or the Arab states.

But beginning with the presidency of John F. Kennedy (1961–1963), the United States began to ignore the Tripartite Declaration and supply more advanced weapons systems, including offensive weapons, to its allies. There were several reasons for this policy shift: Moscow's willingness to sell arms to Egypt, Syria, and then Iraq; the threat Egypt posed to American allies Saudi Arabia and Jordan; and continuous Israeli requests for arms.

As the Arab-Israeli conflict intensified throughout the decade, American arms sales to Israel, in particular, contributed to an increasingly volatile situation. While the Soviet Union continued to supply Egypt with arms, Israel obtained from the United States sophisticated surface-to-air missiles; offensive

An American-made Hawk missile is fired. In 1962 President John F. Kennedy decided to sell the advanced surface-to-air missiles to Israel.

ground-to-ground missiles and battle tanks; and, later, advanced F-4 Phantom fighter planes.

For both superpowers, arms sales served several purposes. First, they helped garner influence with allies (though the Middle Eastern states frequently disregarded their patrons' wishes). Second, arms sales helped friendly states defend themselves against regional adversaries backed by the other superpower. Third, arms sales generated cash, which was especially important to the Soviet Union.

The Six-Day War

The regional arms race contributed to the outbreak of another Arab-Israeli war, in June 1967. The war was the culmination of a series of events that spiraled beyond the control of regional leaders.

Inter-Arab tensions had been increasing over the course of the 1950s and 1960s. Nasser, as leader of the radical camp (which included Syria and Iraq), consistently tried to boost his own nationalist and pan-Arab credentials and hold himself up as the only Arab leader willing to confront Israel.

As its Arab neighbors mobilized to attack in 1967, Israel struck first. Caught by surprise, Egypt, Syria, and Jordan saw their respective air forces obliterated, largely on the ground. Air superiority paved the way for Israel's stunning victory in the Six-Day War. Seen here is the wreckage of an Egyptian fighter jet.

He continually chastised and undermined the conservative camp (the Middle Eastern monarchies, particularly Jordan and Saudi Arabia). Nasser had also made the Palestine question—meaning the establishment of Israel on lands considered rightfully to be part of a Palestinian Arab state—a central part of his campaign for regional leadership. He produced a stream of incendiary rhetoric against Israel.

This might not have been enough to cause war, but Nasser was also being mocked by the Saudis and the Syrians for not doing enough for the Palestine cause. They criticized him for talking about the fight against Israel but not taking any action. The Syrians also accused him of being a tool of the imperialist United States. These accusations took place against a background of confrontation between Israel and Syria.

Israeli-Syrian tensions had begun to increase in the mid-1960s for three reasons: their militaries engaged in occasional skirmishes in the demilitarized zone that had been established between them after the 1947–1949 Arab-Israeli war; Syria tried to divert the headwaters of the Jordan River, which ran through Syria and emptied into Lake Kinneret and which Israel depended on for its water; and Syria provided support for Palestinian guerrilla and terrorist organizations that operated across the Syrian border against Israel. In April 1967 the Syrian and Israeli air forces clashed in Syrian airspace. The following month, Israeli leaders threatened several times to destroy the Syrian regime.

As tensions increased along this front, the Soviet Union became concerned for the security of its ally Syria. In May it sent a report to Nasser that Israel was massing troops along the border with Syria in preparation for an

Israeli soldiers stand guard over a group of Egyptians in the Gaza Strip during the early hours of the Six-Day War, June 5, 1967. The conflict drove Egypt and Syria closer to the Soviet Union while strengthening American ties to Israel.

invasion. Although the report was false, it put Nasser in a difficult position. As the major leader of the Arab world, his credibility and prestige—and Egypt's position as the primary Arab state in the confrontation with Israel—were at stake if he did not react to the report. Other Arab states continued to accuse him of failure and cowardice. The Soviet report galvanized him into action.

In response, Nasser took three measures in quick succession that made war virtually inevitable. On May 14 he sent a large number of Egyptian soldiers into the Sinai Peninsula. Four days later he demanded that the United Nations remove peacekeeping troops who had been stationed in Sinai since the 1956 Suez war. On May 22 he closed the Straits of Tiran, at the entrance to the Gulf of Aqaba, to Israeli shipping. This blocked Israel's access to the Red Sea and shut down its major port of Eilat. Not only were Egyptian troops now within striking distance of Israel, but Israel's economy would also begin to feel a pinch. Nasser's actions were underlined by a unified Arab stance against Israel, as Syria, Egypt, and Jordan signed mutual defense agreements.

All of these developments caused great anxiety among Israeli leaders, who took seriously Arab proclamations that they sought the Jewish state's destruction. The Israelis concluded that they couldn't afford to wait for an Arab attack because, given its small size, Israel was unlikely to survive an assault that penetrated into its territory. Israeli leaders decided to strike first.

On the morning of June 5, Israeli warplanes bombed Egyptian air bases, initiating what would become known as the Six-Day War. Achieving total surprise, the Israeli air force destroyed most of Egypt's warplanes on the ground. Soon Israeli forces engaged Syria and Jordan.

On the ground, the Israel Defense Forces (IDF) completely routed the Egyptian, Syrian, and Jordanian armies. By June 10, when the IDF halted its operations, Israel had taken the Gaza Strip and Sinai Peninsula from Egypt, the Golan Heights from Syria, and the West Bank from Jordan.

Consequences of the War

The Six-Day War represented a stunning military victory for Israel, though it didn't end the Arab-Israeli conflict. It did, however, change the political map of the Middle East. It also had profound implications for Arab-Israeli relations and for Cold War politics.

The war had four main consequences for Israeli-Arab relations and for the superpower competition in the Middle East. First, it led to an unprecedented Soviet involvement in the region. After the devastation of his military, Nasser had no choice but to give in to Soviet demands: in return for arms, Nasser agreed to let Moscow construct and use naval bases along Egypt's Mediterranean coast. Syria, too, needed to rebuild its armed forces, and military aid gave the Soviets significant influence in Damascus.

Second, despite these inroads in Egypt and Syria, the Six-Day War left the Soviet Union in a weaker position vis-à-vis influencing the Arab-Israeli conflict. Because the Soviet Union (and several other Eastern European states) severed diplomatic ties with Israel after the war, Moscow gave up a critical avenue of participation in regional politics. Without ties to Israel, the Soviets had no relevant role to play in Arab-Israeli negotiations; now it was only the United States that could influence Israel in negotiations.

Third, the war led to a strengthening of the American-Israeli relationship. With Egypt and Syria now fully in the Soviet camp, Washington saw no choice but to support Israel in order to counterbalance Soviet influence. The United States became fully committed to protecting Israel's security.

Fourth, the war made the Palestinian cause the key issue in Arab-Israeli relations, as well as an important issue in superpower relations. Before the war, Palestinians had lived under Egyptian rule in Gaza and Jordanian rule in the West Bank. Now Palestinians in these areas lived under Israeli rule, and advocates began to promote self-determination for the Palestinian people. For the international community, this was a much more acceptable cause than the destruction of Israel, which had been the Arab world's primary cause before 1967. The Arabs seized on the issue of Palestinians living under Israeli occupation to vilify and isolate Israel in international organizations. This also drew the United States even closer to Israel; often the United States was Israel's sole defender in the United Nations.

Conclusion

The 1960s ended with closer American-Israeli ties and a stronger Soviet presence in the Middle East through Egypt and Syria. But this didn't translate into a more hostile superpower relationship. Despite periodic crises, the decade ended with the advent of superpower détente—the policy of seeking to relax tensions and better manage potential conflicts. This seemed to augur well for the Middle East. But events in the region soon overtook superpower plans and brought the United States and the Soviet Union to their most dangerous Cold War confrontation over the Middle East.

(Opposite) After the United States sold F-4 Phantom jets like the ones shown here to Israel, the Soviet Union provided Egypt with sophisticated air-defense systems. (Right) U.S. secretary of state Henry Kissinger (seated, at left) confers with Egyptian president Anwar Sadat (center) during a round of shuttle diplomacy, August 1975.

4 The 1970s: War and Peace

In the Middle East, the 1970s witnessed another Arab-Israeli war—and an unexpected peace treaty. Throughout the decade, the United States and the Soviet Union pursued détente, seeking to avoid antagonizing one another and to work toward peaceful resolution of their disputes—but events in the Middle East pulled them to the brink of a direct confrontation. The United States gained a key regional ally during the 1970s, but it also lost another important ally.

The War of Attrition

As the 1970s opened, Egypt and Israel were locked in a bitter if limited clash along the Suez Canal. The hostilities—which began early in 1969 with the Egyptian bombardment of defensive positions Israel had constructed following the 1967 Six-Day War—were dubbed the War of Attrition. The Egyptians sought to avenge their earlier humiliation and ultimately remove Israel from Egyptian territory. Israel, however, was not about to give up the Sinai Peninsula without an Egyptian commitment to peace. Neither side pursued a full-scale offensive; they mainly exchanged artillery fire across the Canal, and Israel launched periodic air strikes deeper into Egyptian territory.

Yet by January 1970 Israel appeared to be gaining the upper hand. That month, Nasser secretly flew to Moscow to ask for advanced fighter jets with which Egypt could attack Israeli territory. The Soviets refused. However, they did provide sophisticated air defense systems, Soviet troops to man them, and even Soviet pilots to patrol the area. In addition, more Soviet military advisers and technicians were sent to Egypt, and the Soviet Union began construction of naval facilities at which to dock and repair Soviet vessels.

By the early 1970s, an estimated 15,000 Soviet military advisers and technicians were in Egypt. This, Soviet leaders believed, gave them significant influence over Egyptian policy toward Israel. In the spirit of détente, the Soviets tried to restrain the Egyptians from pursuing an all-out war with Israel. The Soviet Union threw its support behind a U.S.-brokered cease-fire, which finally brought the War of Attrition to an end in August 1970.

A New Egyptian Leader

The following month, Gamal Abdel Nasser died. He was succeeded by Egypt's vice president, Anwar Sadat.

Sadat came to the presidency with a very different outlook on the Arab-Israeli conflict and on the superpowers. Whereas Nasser had focused almost exclusively on foreign affairs in his bid to make Egypt the leader of the Arab world, Sadat turned inward, determined to fix his country's ailing economy and stabilize its deteriorating social and political situations.

The only way to do this, Sadat concluded, was to end the conflict with Israel, regain the Sinai, and ensure the flow of American aid to Egypt. Ending the conflict with Israel was necessary not simply to remove the burden of incessant fighting but also to redirect precious resources from the military to the domestic social budget. Reclaiming the Sinai was critical for Egypt to recover its national pride, and—in order to begin generating revenue again—reopen the Suez Canal to ships and the Sinai to tourists. Obtaining American support was most critical, as Sadat believed the Soviet Union simply did not have the available financial resources to renew Egypt's stagnant economy, and it carried no leverage with Israel, which was necessary in order to end the conflict. Sadat knew that, lacking the charismatic appeal of Nasser, he would have to deliver tangible benefits to Egyptians in order to secure his political position.

Unfortunately for Sadat, neither Israel nor the United States seemed amenable to negotiating an end to the conflict. Israeli leaders were convinced of their country's military invincibility as a result of the stunning victory in the Six-Day War. They believed that it would be several years before the Arabs were ready for another war, so they thought they could afford to wait until Egypt was willing to make major concessions. For their part, American policymakers were unwilling to force the Israelis to the bargaining table.

In light of this, Sadat determined that he would have to take his country to war again with Israel, both to reverse the humiliation of 1967 and to unfreeze the diplomatic process and draw Washington's attention. Sadat realized that Egypt would need more advanced armaments to fight Israel. On May 27, 1971, he signed the Soviet-Egyptian Treaty of Friendship and Cooperation, which ensured the flow of Soviet arms.

Soviet official Nikolai Podgorny (left) and Anwar Sadat sign the Soviet-Egyptian Treaty of Friendship and Cooperation, May 27, 1971.

Yet Soviet officials also pressured Sadat not to go to war. They worried that war between Egypt and Israel would spark a superpower confrontation and undermine détente, from which the Soviet Union derived significant economic benefits. Soviet leaders balked at selling certain offensive weapons to Egypt, and they placed restrictions on some of the weapons they did sell. In July 1972 Sadat dismissed Soviet advisers in Egypt and sent them back to the Soviet Union.

In March 1973, however, the United States sold advanced fighter jets to Israel. This proved to be a windfall for Sadat, since the Soviets refused to let their ally fall behind in the regional arms race. The Soviet Union provided Egypt with sophisticated air-defense systems, as well as ground-to-ground missiles, significantly enhancing Egypt's capacity to wage war. (Soviet arms sales to Egypt's ally Syria were also stepped up.)

Sadat believed that his country was now ready for war with Israel. Egyptian military leaders secretly began planning a coordinated offensive with their Syrian counterparts.

The 1973 October War

The Arabs chose to launch their attack on Yom Kippur, or the Day of Atonement, which is one of the most important holidays in the Jewish faith. On October 6, as Syrian forces struck Israeli positions in the Golan Heights, Egyptian forces attacked in the Sinai along the Suez Canal. The offensive caught Israel—as well as the superpowers—by surprise.

Egyptian and Syrian armored units overran Israeli positions during the first week of the conflict—generally called the October War but known in

Israel as the Yom Kippur War and in the Arab world as the Ramadan War, because it took place during the Muslim holy month of Ramadan. However, an Israeli counteroffensive in the Golan Heights pushed the Syrian forces back. At one point the Israel Defense Forces advanced to within 25 miles (40 km) of Damascus, Syria's capital.

By the middle of the month, the IDF had shifted its focus to the fighting in the Sinai. After Egyptian armored forces were repelled in one of the largest tank battles in history, Israel gained the initiative, pushing past the Suez Canal and driving into Egypt. The Israeli forces were on the verge of cutting off the strategic Cairo-Ismailia highway when, on October 24, a United Nations–sponsored cease-fire went into effect.

The superpowers had tried, unsuccessfully, to negotiate a cease-fire almost as soon as the fighting broke out. After these peacemaking efforts were rejected by the combatants, however, both the Soviet Union and the United States sought to ensure that their allies didn't lose. On October 11 the Soviet Union began to resupply the Egyptian and Syrian militaries. Three days later the United States began sending critically needed supplies to the IDF by air and sea.

As it became obvious that an Israeli victory was all but assured, both superpowers began pushing harder for a cease-fire, Moscow so that its ally Egypt would be spared further devastation and Washington so that it would not be seen as supporting the Israeli destruction of the Arabs. A cease-fire was declared on October 22. But both Egypt and Israel broke the cease-fire, and by the next day Israel had surrounded and trapped the Egyptian Third Army just east of the Suez Canal. Soviet leaders were furious, and they feared that their major ally in the region was about to have its military completely wiped out. This would severely undermine Soviet credibility as a superpower patron and cause considerable damage to the Soviet Union's position in the Middle East.

Accordingly, Soviet leader Leonid Brezhnev sent a message to Washington on October 24, threatening that if the United States didn't force

An Israeli tank in action in the Golan Heights during the October War, 1973. The conflict, which pitted Egypt and Syria against Israel, brought the United States and the Soviet Union unnervingly close to a direct confrontation.

Israel to stop its advances and respect the cease-fire, the Soviet Union would immediately intervene in the conflict. This was a clear threat of a Soviet military attack on Israel.

For the same reason that Moscow couldn't let the Egyptian Third Army be destroyed, Washington couldn't permit the IDF to be attacked by the Soviet Union. In order to demonstrate American determination to oppose any Soviet intervention in the Middle East, the administration of President Richard Nixon decided to raise the readiness status of U.S. military forces to Defense Condition III (DEFCON III) for only the second time in history. For units armed with nuclear weapons, DEFCON III was the highest alert status during peacetime. President Nixon also informed Brezhnev that if Soviet troops landed in the Middle East, the United States would consider it a violation of the Agreement on the Prevention of Nuclear War. That accord, which the United States and the Soviet Union had signed on June 22, 1973, called for the superpowers to avoid situations that might escalate into nuclear war.

After the exchange of threats—which brought the superpowers uncomfortably close to a direct confrontation over the Middle East, and possibly even a nuclear showdown—the Soviets backed down, and Israel abided by the cease-fire. The IDF left the Egyptian Third Army intact.

By January 1974 Egypt and Israel had accepted a United Nations agreement to pull their forces back. The IDF withdrew to positions in the Sinai about 5 miles (8 km) from the east bank of the Suez Canal; the Egyptians pulled back a similar distance from the west bank of the Canal. A U.N. monitoring force occupied the buffer zone between the two armies.

Egypt Turns West

Israel had won another military victory, but it had sustained heavy losses in the October War. Moreover, Israeli confidence had been shaken by the early successes of the Arab forces. In Egypt, meanwhile, the war provided an enormous psychological boost; for the first time, Arab forces had sent the IDF reeling, if only temporarily.

Anwar Sadat had also achieved one of his major goals: he now had the attention of American policymakers, who were determined to prevent the outbreak of another Arab-Israeli war—in large part to avoid another dangerous superpower confrontation. Washington began to take a more vigorous role in promoting a resolution of the Arab-Israeli conflict. Still, U.S. policy on the issue—directed by Secretary of State Henry Kissinger—concentrated on small, incremental progress. Under Kissinger's "shuttle diplomacy"—so called because the secretary of state had to shuttle between regional capitals, as the leaders of Israel and Egypt and Syria refused to meet face-to-face—the hostile states were encouraged to start by disengaging their forces and only then to deal with bigger issues.

It was a diplomatic gamble by Egypt's president that led to a major breakthrough. In November 1977 Sadat visited Jerusalem and—before Israel's parliament, the Knesset—announced his country's desire to "live with [Israel] in permanent peace based on justice."

Sadat desired an agreement that would end the entire Israeli-Arab conflict. But other Arab leaders refused to negotiate with Israel and were furious with Sadat.

In September 1978 President Jimmy Carter hosted talks between Sadat and the Israeli prime minister, Menachem Begin, at the presidential retreat in Camp David, Maryland. After two weeks of discussions, Sadat and Begin agreed to a framework for peace, the Camp David Accords. On March 26, 1979, the two leaders signed an Israeli-Egyptian peace treaty on the lawn of the White House, in Washington, D.C.

It was no accident that President Carter had played a pivotal role in brokering the treaty, whereas Soviet premier Leonid Brezhnev had played no role whatsoever. In 1976 Sadat had renounced the Soviet-Egyptian Treaty of Friendship and Cooperation. Once U.S. policymakers committed to resolving the conflict between Egypt and Israel, there was no reason for Sadat not to join the American side in the Cold War.

Thus, it might be said that the October War's biggest loser was the Soviet Union. It lost its primary ally in the region. It lost the military bases in Egypt,

Historic handshake: Anwar Sadat, Jimmy Carter, and Menachem Begin celebrate the signing of the Israeli-Egyptian peace treaty, March 26, 1979.

as well as the opportunity to use the power of Egypt to influence regional politics. The United States had effectively countered the Soviet threat of direct involvement in the region.

Sadat's decision to make peace with Israel, even in the face of staunch opposition and condemnation from the rest of the Arab world, engendered American gratitude. After 1979 Egypt received approximately $2 billion per year in economic and military aid, making it second only to Israel (which received about $3 billion annually) as the largest recipient of U.S. foreign aid.

Conclusion

The 1970s marked the high point of American influence in the Middle East during the Cold War. During the decade the U.S.-Israeli relationship deepened, and the United States also gained the Arab world's most populous state as a staunch ally. Although the overall Arab-Israeli conflict remained unresolved, without Egypt the Arab states had no realistic hope of again challenging Israel militarily. U.S. status as the dominant outside power in the Middle East was confirmed.

The moment of triumph did not last long, however. Around the time the United States was gaining a permanent ally in Egypt, it was losing another important regional ally. The Cold War competition in the Middle East was far from over. In fact, the decade-long easing of superpower tensions under détente would end abruptly just as the 1970s were coming to a close. The Soviet Union's invasion of a country bordering on the Middle East was the most notable in a series of events that alarmed U.S. policymakers, spurring a determined American response.

استقلال، آزادی، جمهوری اسلامی
جمهوری اسلامی
هستیم

(Opposite) Supporters of Ayatollah Ruhollah Khomeini march in a massive demonstration in Tehran shortly after the exiled cleric's February 1, 1979, return to Iran. (Right) Shah Mohammed Reza Pahlavi shakes hands with an American general during a 1977 visit to the United States. U.S. support for the repressive shah fueled intense anti-Americanism in Iran.

5 The 1980s: Last Throes of the Superpower Struggle

Two events that occurred in the Middle East in 1979 would set the stage for more intense superpower rivalry in the region during the 1980s: the Iranian Revolution and the Soviet invasion of Afghanistan. While Moscow had no hand in the former, U.S. policymakers feared that the Soviet Union might try to exploit the fall of a staunch American ally to make inroads into the oil-rich Persian Gulf. The Soviet invasion of Afghanistan, which came on the heels of the Iranian Revolution, seemed to confirm the subversive intentions of Soviet leaders. The determined American response to this threat would cause the Soviet Union significant difficulties and would, in fact, contribute to the ending of the Cold War.

The Iranian Revolution

Since 1953, when a U.S.-supported coup helped restore Mohammed Reza Pahlavi to the throne, Iran had been one of the most loyal American allies in the Middle East. The so-called Twin Pillars strategy, crafted by the administration of President Richard Nixon, relied on Iran (along with Saudi Arabia) to safeguard U.S. interests in the Persian Gulf and to prevent Soviet infiltration. The shah fulfilled this role—and sought to make his country the foremost power in the region—by purchasing billions of dollars' worth of advanced weapons systems from the United States.

Domestically, however, the shah was a ruthless dictator who brutally repressed those who disagreed with his rule. His secret police, the SAVAK, was loathed and feared by the Iranian people. Through its network of informers, the SAVAK rooted out dissenters, many of whom faced torture and execution.

But the shah's authoritarian rule was just one reason he became increasingly unpopular among his subjects. Heavy spending on the military, combined with attempts at rapid industrialization, caused severe economic problems. Attempts to modernize Iranian society by adopting Western values offended religious conservatives, who believed the shah was denigrating the role of Islam. Poorer Iranians grumbled about the royal family's extravagant lifestyle and its reputation for corruption. And the shah's alliance with the United States—which many Iranians saw as nothing more than a cover for foreign domination—caused widespread anger. In short, by his third decade on the throne, the shah had alienated most segments of Iranian society.

Social and political unrest began increasing by the mid-1970s. The opposition came to be symbolized by Ayatollah Ruhollah Khomeini, an exiled cleric who called for the violent overthrow of the shah. Khomeini was an avowed Islamist—he wanted to transform Iranian government and society in accordance with his interpretation of Islamic law. Although not all opponents of the shah shared this conservative religious agenda, Khomeini drew support from millions of poor Iranians, students, and others who felt alienated and isolated by the regime's economic and political policies.

In 1978 discontent boiled over into large demonstrations on the streets of Iranian cities. As these protests grew increasingly violent, the shah ordered a crackdown. On September 8, 1978, hundreds of Iranians were killed as the shah's troops fired on crowds in Tehran. This merely increased popular anger, and the protests continued through the rest of the year.

The shah was forced into exile in January 1979, but the turmoil continued. On February 1 Khomeini returned from exile in France, galvanizing his supporters. Over the following weeks, the remnants of support for the shah disintegrated, and Khomeini and his Islamist allies seized power (though they did not completely consolidate their rule for several years). On April 1, 1979, the Islamic Republic of Iran was proclaimed. Its fundamentalist theocratic government sought to ensure that Islam would be the framework for the organization of all political and social life.

U.S.-Iranian relations deteriorated quickly. The Islamists made no secret of their contempt for the United States, which Khomeini would dub "the Great Satan." In November 1979 a group of Islamic militant students—with encouragement from, or at least the tacit approval of, the Iranian government—stormed the U.S. embassy in Tehran and took American diplomats and staff hostage. The United States slapped economic sanctions on Iran, but 52 Americans would be held hostage for 444 days.

Radical Iranian students parade a bound and blindfolded American hostage before the cameras after their takeover of the U.S. embassy in Tehran, November 1979.

As a result of the Iranian Revolution, the United States lost one of its most important allies in the Middle East. Furthermore, the Carter administration's inability to win the hostages' release—through diplomatic pressure or by means of a military operation in April 1980—undermined American prestige.

Yet the U.S. loss wasn't necessarily the Soviet Union's gain. The Islamic Republic was vehemently anti-Communist. Its leaders had no interest in aligning with either superpower. They did, however, seek to export their revolution to neighboring Muslim countries—including important American allies such as Saudi Arabia—whose regimes they branded impious and un-Islamic.

Tehran's criticism of its neighbors was underpinned by an important sectarian distinction. Iran's ruling regime, and the overwhelming majority of the country's population, followed the Shia branch of Islam; most other countries in the region were majority Sunni. Followers of Islam's two largest branches had a centuries-long history of antagonism toward each other.

The Soviet Invasion of Afghanistan

On December 25, 1979, Soviet military aircraft began flying combat units of the Red Army into Afghanistan. These elite soldiers were the vanguard of a large Soviet invasion force. By year's end, that invasion force would topple the unpopular Communist regime of Hafizullah Amin, install another Communist regime under Babrak Karmal, and occupy the rugged, mountainous country along the border with the Soviet Union's Central Asian republics.

By 1987, when this photograph of Red Army soldiers near Kabul was taken, the Soviet occupation of Afghanistan had entered its eighth year. Moscow's decision to invade its southern neighbor had proved a disastrous blunder.

Soviet leaders decided to invade Afghanistan somewhat reluctantly. The country had a long history of ethnic and factional fighting. A delicate balance in Afghan politics was disturbed in April 1978, when a small Communist group overthrew the regime of President Mohammed Daud Khan. While friendly toward Moscow, the Communists proceeded to badly mismanage governance. In particular, their effort to impose a Marxist framework on socially conservative Afghanistan generated intense opposition. The new government faced a series of demonstrations and uprisings that threatened to bring it down. Soviet policymakers feared a loss of influence in Afghanistan, and they also worried that instability in Afghanistan would spill over into the Soviet Central Asian republics.

If the invasion was primarily an attempt by Moscow to install a stable and friendly government along the borders of the Soviet Union, that was not how it was perceived in Washington. American policymakers regarded the Soviet actions as an aggressive attempt at Communist expansion, the opening move of a major thrust into the Middle East. Officials in the Carter administration worried that the Soviet Union might try to exploit post-revolution instability in Iran and alter the balance of power in the region.

The Carter Doctrine

In his 1980 State of the Union Address, delivered on January 23, President Carter made clear that his administration considered the Soviet invasion of Afghanistan a threat to the stability of the Persian Gulf region, and hence as a huge threat to American interests. "The region which is now threatened by Soviet troops in Afghanistan," Carter said, "is of great strategic importance: It contains more than two-thirds of the world's exportable oil. The Soviet effort to dominate Afghanistan has brought Soviet military forces to within 300 miles of the Indian Ocean and close to the Straits of Hormuz, a waterway through which most of the world's oil must flow. The Soviet Union is now attempting to consolidate a strategic position, therefore, that poses a grave threat to the free movement of Middle East oil."

The president indicated that the United States would respond vigorously to this threat, articulating what came to be called the Carter Doctrine. "Let our position be absolutely clear: An attempt by any outside force to gain control of the Persian Gulf region will be regarded as an assault on the vital interests of the United States of America, and such an assault will be repelled by any means necessary, including military force," the president declared. It was the most forceful American policy regarding the Middle East since the 1957 Eisenhower Doctrine.

"Holy Warriors"

If the Carter administration publicly warned the Soviet leadership against further Middle East interventions, it also secretly worked to roll back the Soviet occupation of Afghanistan. It did this by funding Afghan resistance

During the Soviet occupation of Afghanistan, the United States funneled millions of dollars in military aid to Afghan resistance fighters known as the mujahideen. In this photo, a mujahideen fighter takes aim at a Soviet aircraft with a deadly U.S. Stinger missile.

fighters known as the mujahideen (or "holy warriors"). Through neighboring Pakistan, the CIA funneled money and arms to the mujahideen, who as devout Muslims were especially offended by Soviet atheism. Soon Muslims from other countries began making their way to Afghanistan to join in the jihad, or holy war, against the Soviets. Muslim countries such as Saudi Arabia also provided material support to the anti-Soviet resistance.

In 1980 President Carter was defeated in his bid for reelection, in part because of his failure to secure the release of the American hostages being held in Iran. His successor, Ronald Reagan, came to office determined to take a hard line against the Soviet Union. Thus Reagan is said to have ushered in the period of the "second Cold War."

Reagan dramatically increased the overall U.S. defense budget, and throughout the world he supported groups battling Communist regimes. In Afghanistan aid to the mujahideen was ramped up, from an estimated $30 million in 1980 to $250 million in 1985 and more than $625 million in 1987.

By the mid-1980s Soviet forces had become bogged down in Afghanistan. Unable to quell the U.S.- and Saudi-funded mujahideen, the Soviets were sustaining heavy casualties, and morale in the Red Army had plummeted. In addition, the occupation of Afghanistan was costing as much as $5 billion annually, a sum the economically stressed Soviet Union could ill afford to pay.

The Iran-Iraq War

Even as U.S.-sponsored fighters were bleeding the Soviets in Afghanistan, the superpowers found themselves on the same side of another Middle Eastern conflict: the Iran-Iraq War, which lasted from 1980 until 1988.

For decades, Iran and Iraq had been rivals for regional leadership. Historical antagonisms between the Shia and Persian culture represented by Iran and the Sunni and Arab culture represented by Iraq extended back centuries. While a contentious border dispute between the two countries was apparently settled in 1975, when the Algiers Accord fixed the Iran-Iraq boundary down the middle of the Shatt al Arab waterway, neither side was completely happy with the arrangement. Because the Shatt al Arab provides Iraq's major outlet to the Persian Gulf, Iraqi leaders would have preferred to control the entire waterway.

Two events in 1979 helped set the stage for war between the rival countries: Iran's Islamic Revolution and the consolidation of power in Iraq by Saddam Hussein. In July, Saddam—who as vice president had long been in charge of internal security in Iraq—eased out President Ahmed Hassan al-Bakr, made himself president, and launched a brutal purge of the ruling Baath Party. Iran's religious leaders immediately began criticizing Saddam's secular and socialist-oriented regime as un-Islamic. Worse from Saddam's perspective, they began fomenting unrest among Iraq's majority Shiite population.

Saddam therefore regarded the Islamic Revolution in Iran as a threat to his Sunni-dominated regime. But he also sensed an opportunity. In the wake of the revolution, Iran continued to suffer significant internal disorder as Khomeini's religious government struggled to consolidate its authority. Beginning in November, Tehran also faced a deepening confrontation with the United States over the American hostages. Saddam calculated that Iran would be ill prepared to mount an effective defense against an Iraqi invasion. He believed he could seize full control of the Shatt al Arab, as well as much of Iran's oil-producing Khuzestan Province, whose large Arab population he expected to rally to his cause.

On September 22, 1980, Iraqi forces invaded Iran. In the first weeks of the war, Saddam's calculations appeared to have been correct. His army drove deep into Khuzestan. But Iranian resistance stiffened, and by the end of the year the Iraqi advance had been halted.

Iranian forces counterattacked, gradually pushing the Iraqis back. By the summer of 1982, the Iranians crossed into Iraqi territory for the first time since the start of the war. The fighting was brutal and produced massive casualties on both sides. But Iran, whose much larger population enabled it to mount "human wave" attacks, slowly appeared to be gaining the upper hand.

Neither of the superpowers wanted to see an Iranian victory. Iraq was one of the Soviet Union's few remaining allies in the Middle East. Moreover, Iran's Islamic ideology was fervently anti-Communist. Thus the Soviet Union provided Iraq with vast quantities of military equipment with which to fight Iran. In Washington, anger over the hostage crisis of 1979–1981 lingered, and American policymakers feared that Iran's Islamic extremism might undermine the governments of key American allies in the Persian Gulf area. From about 1982, American policy favored Iraq. Yet because Iraq was a fierce opponent of Israel and a clear Soviet ally, Washington did not want to see a complete Iraqi victory, either. Its preferred outcome was for Iraq and Iran to exhaust each other to the point where both would be too weak to threaten American interests. Thus the aid that the United States provided to Iraq—intelligence on Iranian troop movements, technical assistance, and

An Iraqi soldier walks past the bodies of Iranians killed in battle during the Iran-Iraq War. Although Iraq was an ally of the Soviet Union, U.S. policy also came to favor Iraq during the eight-year-long conflict, largely because American officials feared that an Iranian victory could spread Islamic extremism throughout the Persian Gulf.

limited military supplies—was intended to enable Saddam to stave off defeat but not gain a decisive advantage.

As Iraq's oil industry faltered during the war, however, Saddam came increasingly to rely on American allies Saudi Arabia and Kuwait to fund his war against Iran. Iraq therefore needed to retain American goodwill, and so it became less vocal in its opposition to Israel and, in 1984, restored diplomatic ties with the United States. (Those ties had been severed in 1967, after the Six-Day War.)

The Iran-Iraq War dragged on. Iraq introduced chemical weapons onto the battlefield, and both sides targeted enemy cities with missile attacks. Yet the conflict remained stalemated. Finally, in August of 1988, a cease-fire arranged by the United Nations ended the fighting. Combined, Iran and Iraq had suffered more than a million casualties during the eight-year conflict.

Conclusion

Around the time the Iran-Iraq War was winding down, the Soviet Union—unable to quash resistance from the mujahideen in Afghanistan and facing increasing difficulties at home—began withdrawing its troops from Afghanistan. By February of 1989 that withdrawal was complete.

The 1980s, which had begun with the American position in the Middle East seemingly threatened, would end with the United States as the region's undisputed outside power. In fact, the Cold War itself was all but over, and in its aftermath the United States would be the world's lone superpower.

By the late 1980s, the Cold War had wound down. (Opposite) U.S. president Ronald Reagan shakes hands with Soviet leader Mikhail Gorbachev after the signing of a nuclear-missile treaty, 1988. (Right) Germans celebrate the fall of the Berlin Wall, November 9, 1989.

6 Conclusion: The End of the Cold War

It is impossible to attribute the end of the Cold War to a single event or cause. However, many historians believe an important turning point occurred in 1985, when Mikhail Gorbachev came to power in the Soviet Union. Gorbachev was determined to reform Soviet communism, both by permitting more openness and freedoms in Soviet society and by restructuring the faltering Soviet economy. He recognized that to achieve these goals, the Soviet Union would have to divert economic resources from the military to the civilian sector. This would mean not only extricating the Red Army from the quagmire in Afghanistan, but also scaling back the entire Cold War confrontation with the United States. The Soviet Union simply could not keep pace with American military spending.

Ultimately, Gorbachev's incremental reforms created a momentum that was beyond his ability to control. As small political and economic freedoms were allowed, the Soviet population began to demand more.

The Cold War competition in the Middle East ended without a direct military clash between the United States and the Soviet Union, which would likely have proved catastrophic. Yet the superpowers did leave a troubled legacy in the region. Some of the most notorious Islamist terrorists, including Osama bin Laden (pictured here), developed their philosophy of jihad during the war against Soviet occupation in Afghanistan—a war funded in part by the United States.

Meanwhile, Soviet control over the countries of Eastern Europe was relaxed. In 1989 the Communist regimes of these countries fell in a series of mostly peaceful revolutions. On November 9, 1989, the Berlin Wall—for many the ultimate symbol of the Cold War division—was breached.

Hard-line Soviet Communists tried to halt the reforms by ousting Gorbachev in an August 1991 coup. But by then it was too late. Within a few days, the coup had failed. By the end of the year the Soviet Union had ceased to exist, and with its passing the Cold War was over.

* * * * *

Remarkably, the Soviet Union and the United States had, for 45 years, avoided a direct clash over the Middle East—despite at least one close call and the existence of competing vital interests for both countries. The leaders of the superpowers were well aware that a direct military confrontation might spiral into a general nuclear war. Both sides sought to avoid this, if necessary by reining in their allies.

Thus it might be argued that, despite their bitter rivalry, the United States and the Soviet Union acted rationally in the Middle East during the Cold War. Perhaps this, rather than the conflicts and divisions they engendered, should be the superpowers' legacy in the region.

1938: Oil is discovered in Saudi Arabia, leading to a long-standing American commitment to the country.

1941: British and Soviet forces occupy Iran and, in September, overthrow the shah to prevent him from supporting Nazi Germany.

1945: The Soviets back the declaration of an independent state in Iranian Azerbaijan. The Soviet Union demands that Turkey return the eastern Turkish areas of Kars and Ardahan; later the Soviets demand that Turkey allow them to build a military base at the Turkish Straits.

1946: In May, under increasing Iranian and American pressure, Soviet troops finally leave Iran.

1947: In a speech before the U.S. Congress, President Harry Truman proclaims what comes to be known as the Truman Doctrine, offering aid to Greece and Turkey and to any other country that requested help in fending off Communist advances.

1948: Israel is established on May 14.

1950: Britain, France, and the United States issue the Tripartite Declaration, in which they announce they will maintain a balance of power between Arabs and Israelis by strict control over arms sales to the region.

1951: The Iranian oil industry is nationalized.

1952: The Free Officers, a group of Egyptian military officers led by Gamal Abdel Nasser, overthrow the monarchy in Egypt.

1953: Mohammad Mossadeq, Iran's prime minister, is overthrown in a coup sponsored by the U.S. Central Intelligence Agency.

1955: The Soviet Union—through its Eastern European satellite Czechoslovakia—sells advanced arms to Egypt.

1956: Egypt nationalizes the Suez Canal in July. In late October, Israeli troops invade Egypt's Sinai Peninsula; using the threat to Suez Canal shipping as a pretext, British and French forces attack Egyptian positions in early November. Under Soviet threats and American pressure, the British and French forces withdraw by the end of the year (Israeli forces pull out the following March).

1957: In January President Dwight D. Eisenhower outlines the Eisenhower Doctrine, which declares that the United States will give aid, including American military support, to any Middle Eastern state resisting attacks by Communist countries. In July the doctrine is used to justify sending U.S. Marines to Lebanon.

1965: All U.S. aid to Egypt is discontinued, forcing President Nasser to turn to the Soviet Union.

1967: In June Israel routs the combined militaries of Egypt, Syria, and Jordan, conquering the Gaza Strip, Sinai Peninsula, Golan Heights, and West Bank in what comes to be called the Six-Day War.

1970: Nasser dies in September and is succeeded by Anwar Sadat.

1971: The Soviet-Egyptian Treaty of Friendship and Cooperation is signed.

1973: On October 6, Egypt and Syria attack Israel, touching off a three-week conflict widely known as the October War (it is called the Yom Kippur War by Israelis and the Ramadan War by Arabs). After Egypt's Third Army is surrounded and faced with annihilation, the Soviet Union threatens to intervene directly, and the U.S. military alert status is raised to

DEFCON III, sparking fears of a direct superpower confrontation.

1978: Opposition to the U.S.-backed shah mounts in Iran. With mediation from U.S. president Jimmy Carter, Egyptian president Anwar Sadat and Israeli prime minister Menachem Begin agree to a framework for peace, the Camp David Accords, in September.

1979: In January the shah of Iran goes into exile; on February 1 the exiled Shiite cleric Ayatollah Ruhollah Khomeini returns to Tehran to a tumultuous welcome. On March 26 an Egyptian-Israeli peace treaty is signed in Washington, D.C. On April 1 the Islamic Republic of Iran is proclaimed. In July Iraqi vice president Saddam Hussein makes himself president and purges the ruling party. In November radical Iranian students overrun the U.S. embassy in Tehran and take its personnel hostage. In December Soviet troops invade Afghanistan.

1980: On January 23 President Carter announces what comes to be called the Carter Doctrine, which says that any attempt by a hostile power to take control of Persian Gulf oil will be considered a direct attack on vital American interests. In April a U.S. military operation to rescue the American hostages in Iran has to be aborted. On September 22, Iraqi forces invade Iran, touching off the eight-year-long Iran-Iraq War.

1981: U.S. hostages held in Iran since November 1979 are finally released.

1985: Mikhail Gorbachev comes to power in the Soviet Union.

1988: Soviet troops begin withdrawing from Afghanistan after a costly decade-long occupation.

1991: A coup attempt against Gorbachev in August fails. In December the Soviet Union collapses.

capitalism—an economic system characterized by private ownership of factories and businesses, in which market forces determine which goods are produced and how much they cost.

Cold War—the global ideological and strategic struggle between the United States and the Soviet Union, which lasted from the late 1940s until 1991.

colonialism—control or domination by one country over an area or people outside its boundaries; the policy of colonizing foreign lands.

communism—a political and economic system under which all property and the means of production are controlled by the state, which in theory distributes goods fairly to all citizens.

détente—the practice of trying to ease strained relations between states; specifically, the period of lessened tensions between the United States and the Soviet Union from the late 1960s to 1979.

Islamist—a person who desires that government and society be reordered to conform to Islamic law.

northern tier—the northern geographical boundaries of the Middle East (the term usually denotes Turkey and Iran, though sometimes Afghanistan is also included).

pan-Arab—involving or appealing to all Arabs; advocating the political union of all Arab countries.

Shia—a denomination of Islam that is followed by an estimated 15 percent of Muslims worldwide but that claims a majority of believers in Iran and Iraq.

Sunni—the dominant sect in Islam, which is followed by an estimated 85 percent of Muslims worldwide.

superpower—one of a small number of dominant states during a historical era; in the Cold War context, either the Soviet Union or the United States.

Further Reading

Bass, Warren. *Support Any Friend: Kennedy's Middle East and the Making of the U.S.-Israel Alliance.* Oxford, UK: Oxford University Press, 2003.

Bickerton, Ian J., and Carla L. Klausner. *A History of the Arab-Israeli Conflict.* 5th edition. Upper Saddle River, N.J.: Prentice Hall, 2007.

Dobson, Alan P., and Steve Marsh. *US Foreign Policy Since 1945.* London: Routledge, 2001.

Gaddis, John Lewis. *The Cold War: A New History.* New York: Penguin Press, 2005.

Gerges, Fawaz A. *The Superpowers and the Middle East: Regional and International Politics, 1955–1967.* Boulder, Colo.: Westview Press, 1994.

Golan, Galia. *Soviet Policies in the Middle East: From World War II to Gorbachev.* Cambridge, UK: Cambridge University Press, 1990.

Kuniholm, Bruce R. *The Origins of the Cold War in the Near East: Great Power Conflict and Diplomacy in Iran, Turkey, and Greece.* Princeton, N.J.: Princeton University Press, 1994.

Quandt, William B. *Peace Process: American Diplomacy and the Arab-Israeli Conflict Since 1967.* Revised edition. Washington, D.C.: Brookings Institution Press, 2001.

Raviv, Dan, and Yossi Melman. *Friends in Deed: Inside the U.S.-Israel Alliance.* New York: Hyperion, 1994.

http://www.haaretz.com

English-language Web site of *Haaretz*, a widely respected newspaper in Israel, published in both English and Hebrew.

http://www.arabicnews.com

An English-language Web site compiling news from all over the Arab world.

http://meria.idc.ac.il

Middle East Review of International Affairs provides a series of in-depth analytical articles dealing with contemporary and historical Middle Eastern issues. It also includes links to other resources.

http://www.wilsoncenter.org/index.cfm?topic_id=1409&fuseaction=topics.home

Web site of the Cold War International History Project, a joint effort housed at the Woodrow Wilson International Center for Scholars. It includes a comprehensive and constantly updated archive of the Cold War.

http://menic.utexas.edu/menic.html

The Middle East Network Information Center is a coordinating body providing links to numerous other databases and Web sites dealing with a wide range of issues related to Middle East politics.

Index

Numbers in ***bold italic*** refer to captions.

Contributors

Brent E. Sasley is assistant professor at the University of Texas at Arlington. He received his Ph.D. from McGill University, in Montreal. He has lectured and written widely on the Middle East, with a special focus on Israeli and Turkish politics. His previous co-edited book, *Redefining Security in the Middle East*, dealt with emerging security issues in the region.

Picture Credits

Page:
2: Robert Nickelsberg/Getty Images
6: S.M. Amin/Saudi Aramco World/PADIA
7: Photo 491642008(256) in The Franklin D. Roosevelt Presidential Library, New York
10: © OTTN Publishing
13: Library of Congress
15: Library of Congress
18: Associated Press
19: Associated Press
20: Keystone/Stringer/Getty Images
23: Staff/AFP/Getty Images
25: G. Godden/Stringer/Getty Images
26: Library of Congress
30: Howard Sochurek/Time Life Pictures/Getty Images
31: Associated Press
35: Ted Gomes/Department of Defense
36: Associated Press
38: David Rubinger/Time & Life Pictures/Getty Images
42: TSGT Brad Fallin/Department of Defense
43: Harry Koundakjian/Associated Press
46: Associated Press
49: David Rubinger/Time Life Pictures/Getty Images
52: Associated Press
54: Saris/Associated Press
55: MSGT Denham, USAF/Department of Defense
58: MPI/Getty Images
60: Bob Martin/Associated Press
62: Robert Nickelsberg/Liaison/Getty Images
66: William Foley/Time Life Pictures/Getty Images
68: Ronald Reagan Presidential Library
69: SSGT. F. Lee Corkran/Department of Defense
70: Federal Bureau of Investigation

Cover photos: Main Photo: AFP/AFP/Getty Images
Bottom Photos: SSGT Joceyln Rich, USAF; Hulton Archive/Getty Images; Keystone/Getty Images